Nelson

Minna Lacey

Illustrated by David Cuzik

Contents

Chapter 1 Off to sea   5

Chapter 2 Growing up in Norfolk   10

Chapter 3 Life on board   14

Chapter 4 Rising up the ranks   19

Chapter 5 Nelson's first big victory   24

Chapter 6 Wounded at Tenerife   31

Chapter 7 The Battle of the Nile   36

Chapter 8 Lady Emma Hamilton   41

Chapter 9 The Battle of Copenhagen   47

Chapter 10 Victory at Trafalgar   53

History consultant: Colin White - National Maritime Museum,
Greenwich, & Royal Naval Museum, Portsmouth

Reading consultant: Alison Kelly - Roehampton University

Series editors: Lesley Sims and Jane Chisholm
Designed by Russell Punter

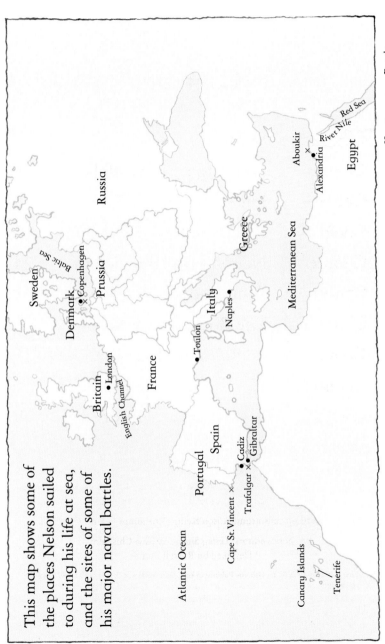

This map shows some of the places Nelson sailed to during his life at sea, and the sites of some of his major naval battles.

Key to map: × Battle

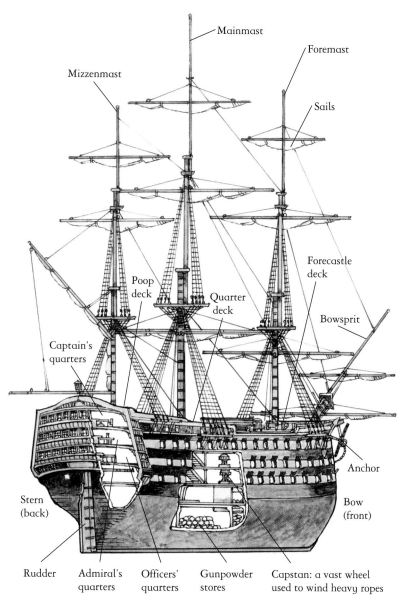

Mainmast

Foremast

Mizzenmast

Sails

Forecastle
deck

Poop
deck

Quarter
deck

Bowsprit

Captain's
quarters

Anchor

Stern
(back)

Bow
(front)

Rudder

Admiral's
quarters

Officers'
quarters

Gunpowder
stores

Capstan: a vast wheel
used to wind heavy ropes

Nelson spent most of his life sailing and eventually
commanding great warships, like this one.

Chapter 1

Off to sea

As the stagecoach for Chatham docks started moving, Horatio Nelson jumped on board and gave his father a final wave. At just 12 years old, he was off on his own to join his uncle's warship, the *Raisonnable*, and about to start a great adventure.

"Goodbye!" he yelled from the window. "I'll write soon."

Six hours later, the coach arrived at Chatham. Horatio looked around anxiously, hoping to see his uncle, but there was no one to meet him. So he picked up his bag and wandered down the cobbled lane to the docks.

It was a bitterly cold morning in March, 1771, and there were boats and sailors everywhere. Feeling thoroughly exhausted after the journey, Horatio plucked up his courage and approached a man in a naval officer's uniform.

"Please could you help me, sir?" he asked. "I'm looking for the *Raisonnable*."

The officer nodded in the direction of a large ship. "She's moored over there. I'll find someone to row you over."

As he sat in a rowing boat, heading for the *Raisonnable*, Horatio gazed in awe at the 64-gun warship towering out of the water. The tiny boat pulled up alongside the vast ship. Grabbing hold of a slippery rope ladder, Horatio scrambled up the side.

On board he was caught up in a whirlwind of activity. Sailors rushed this way and that, shouting orders, scrubbing, painting and polishing, mending ropes and loading barrels.

An officer checked his name on a list. "Ah yes, Midshipman Nelson. This way."

He led Horatio down some steep steps into the depths of the ship, until they were below the waterline. It was terribly gloomy, with just a few glimmering lanterns hanging from the beams.

The timbers creaked as the ship rocked to and fro and the air smelled of damp and tar. His stomach churning, Horatio started to feel sick.

The officer showed him a sea chest for his belongings and a very narrow space for his hammock.

"Can I see my uncle, Captain Suckling, now sir?" Horatio asked.

"I'm afraid not. Captain Suckling won't be here for another week," the officer replied.

Horatio's heart sank. He suddenly felt very small and lonely, and far away from home...

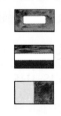

Chapter 2

Growing up in Norfolk

Nelson's home was a small village called Burnham Thorpe in Norfolk, not far from the sea. His father was priest of the local church and, although the family had a comfortable home, they weren't rich.

Horatio spent hours exploring the creeks and dunes by the coast, watching the fishing

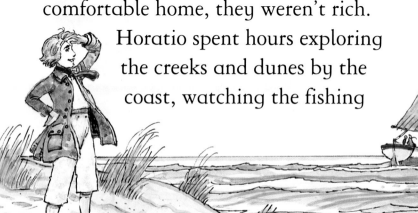

boats and trading ships as they sailed out to sea. Then something happened that was to change his life forever. When Horatio was just nine, his mother died, leaving his father with eight children to bring up alone, the youngest only a baby.

Horatio's uncle Maurice came to visit to see how he could help. He strode into the garden where the children were playing and spotted Horatio, who looked small and weak for his age, wrestling with his older brother William.

"Shouldn't we stop them?" Maurice asked Susannah, Horatio's older sister. "Horatio might get hurt."

"Oh, don't worry about him," Susannah laughed. "He's much tougher than he looks. It's usually William who runs off crying."

The children were eager to hear Maurice's stories of life at sea.

"Tell us how you attacked those French ships in the Caribbean," Horatio begged.

Maurice grinned with delight and told them of his adventures, clashing swords with fierce enemies across the ocean. Horatio was spellbound.

Maurice offered to help with the children's education and, shortly after his visit, Horatio and his brothers were sent to boarding school in nearby North Walsham.

Three years later, while Horatio was home for the summer, he read in the newspaper about a war between Britain and Spain in the South Atlantic.

"It says here that Uncle Maurice has been made captain of the warship *H.M.S. Raisonnable*," he told his brother William, with great excitement. "The ship sets sail from Chatham in the next few weeks."

At once, Horatio wrote to his uncle asking for a job...

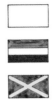

Chapter 3

Life on board

By the time his uncle boarded the *Raisonnable*, Midshipman Nelson was growing used to the strange wooden world that had become his home.

As the ship sat in the port, waiting for the order to sail, Nelson was learning how to be a sailor. He clambered up the rigging, hoisted and set sails, heaved cannons into position, tied knots and pushed the capstan – the mighty wheel used to wind ropes and cables.

But some parts of life on board terrified him. One sailor caught stealing was flogged with the hated whip, the cat-o-nine-tails, until his back was red with blood. After the beating, his wounds were covered with salt, which made him howl even more.

Every day, new provisions arrived which had to be stored on the ship. There were barrels of beer, wine, rum and water, as well as crates of salt beef, pork, bread, oatmeal, raisins, biscuits and cheese. Live chickens, pigs, goats and ducks were kept on board too.

Nelson ate with the other sailors on tables in the lower gun deck. Breakfast was usually porridge, with salt beef stew for lunch, and biscuits and cheese for supper. To drink there was beer or grog, a mixture of rum and water.

When Captain Suckling arrived, Nelson was hugely relieved. His uncle was happy to show him how to read maps of the ocean and calculate the ship's position. Then news came from the Admiralty, Britain's naval headquarters in London, that the war was over. The *Raisonnable* would not be sailing after all. Instead, Nelson found work on a merchant boat heading for the West Indies.

Over the next six years he barely set foot on land at all, crossing the world on many different ships. He became a superb navigator, but he could also be fiercely stubborn and independent.

On an expedition to the Arctic, Nelson secretly left his ship one night to hunt on the ice for a polar bear. He was armed only with a musket – and he knew the captain would be cross that he had left the ship without permission – but he was determined to bring back a bearskin for his father. Climbing an icy ridge, he came face to face with a bear.

The captain was furious when he found out. "Fire a blank from the cannon," he shouted. The blast scared the bear away and Nelson returned empty-handed, to a severe telling-off.

On another voyage to the Far East, Nelson grew dangerously sick with malaria. As he lay feverish in his hammock, he thought he saw a glowing orb hanging in the air before him.

"It's a sign..." he thought. "A sign that I will do incredible things for my country. I am destined to become a great leader."

Chapter 4

Rising up the ranks

At 18, Horatio passed the exam to become a lieutenant, the first rank of officer in the Royal Navy. Soon after that, he found work aboard a small warship called the *Lowestoffe*, bound for the West Indies.

It was 1777 and the American colonies, supported by France, were fighting a war against Britain for independence.

One stormy night, the captain of the *Lowestoffe* caught sight of an American merchant ship ahead. "Prepare to board the prize!" Captain Locker ordered his second-in-command, as they drew close.

"It's too dangerous sir," the officer argued. To board the ship, they would have to row over to it in a smaller boat, a difficult task in rough seas.

"Is there no one on board who can capture the enemy vessel?" Locker yelled to his crew.

Seizing the opportunity, Nelson quickly leaped into the rowing boat. With great skill, he pulled alongside the merchant ship and climbed aboard, taking command.

"Bravo!" Locker boomed in delight.

Nelson's daring and bravery was highly praised by his senior officers and over the next few years his promotion was rapid. By the time he was 21 he had become the youngest captain in the Royal Navy.

In 1785, while sailing in the Caribbean, Nelson met a pretty widow named Fanny Nisbet, and her young son, Josiah. Nelson fell in love with Fanny and asked her to marry him. Their wedding took place on the island of Nevis in March 1787 and, soon after, they moved to London. But Fanny was unhappy there – it was cold and dirty and full of smog. So the couple moved to Norfolk to live with Nelson's father in Burnham Thorpe.

Britain was now at peace and with no battles to be fought Nelson found himself out of a job. He spent his time studying his sea charts, working in the garden and writing endless letters to the Admiralty asking for work. He also followed, with horror, dramatic events unfolding in France.

"An army of French peasants has stormed the Bastille prison in Paris," he read out of the newspaper to his father and Fanny. "They're demanding a revolution. All of France is in uproar. The royal family fear for their lives."

Over the next few years, French revolutionaries captured and beheaded the French king, Louis XVI and his wife, Marie Antoinette, along

with hundreds of nobles. The rebels planned to start similar uprisings in other countries – including Britain.

War was declared between Britain and France and at last Nelson was sent to sea, to keep an eye on the activities of the French fleet in the Mediterranean.

While on duty, Nelson stopped off in Naples, a large port in Italy, and visited the British ambassador, Sir William Hamilton. He found the elderly man helpful and interesting and they became good friends. Nelson was also impressed by Sir William's charming – and much younger – second wife, Lady Emma Hamilton.

Chapter 5

Nelson's first big victory

By 1795, Nelson was becoming aware of a major new threat in the Mediterranean. The French army was led by a brilliant young general, Napoleon Bonaparte, who appeared set on conquering Europe.

Napoleon was currently storming into northern Italy. News came that he had taken Milan, and had Spain, Holland and Prussia on his side too. Fear spread that he would invade Britain next and no one would be able to stop him. But Nelson thought this was nonsense.

"Napoleon will never get his troops across the channel without beating our Navy first," he declared. "And we shall never let that happen."

Now Britain was at war with Spain as well as France, it was too dangerous for the British fleet to stay in the Mediterranean. So, early in 1797, Nelson – Commodore of the ship the *Captain* – was ordered to sail back to England.

On reaching Gibraltar, he learned that the Spanish fleet had left for the Atlantic four days earlier. Soon after that, the *Captain* sailed into thick fog.

As it began to clear, Nelson made out several huge warships nearby. "Pass me my telescope," he called to a young officer, Thomas Hardy. Nelson was horrified to discover the ships were Spanish. "We're surrounded by the enemy," he announced.

"But they'll destroy us!" cried Hardy.

"Don't worry," Nelson replied. "It's still foggy. We'll sail right past them. With luck, they won't even notice."

Showing nerves of steel, Nelson steered his ship through the middle of the enemy fleet and escaped.

He caught up with the British fleet near Cape St. Vincent off Portugal and reported what he had seen to Admiral Sir John Jervis, commander-in-chief of the Mediterranean fleet.

"We'll sail between them and attack each group in turn," Jervis decided.

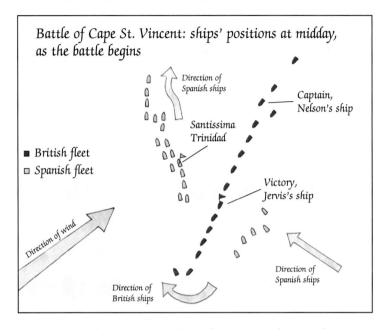

Battle of Cape St. Vincent: ships' positions at midday, as the battle begins

Direction of Spanish ships

Captain, Nelson's ship

Santissima Trinidad

■ British fleet
□ Spanish fleet

Victory, Jervis's ship

Direction of wind

Direction of Spanish ships

Direction of British ships

Once the battle had started, Nelson saw some Spanish ships escaping. Fearing that victory might slip away from them, he broke out of the battle formation and steered over to the mighty 130-gun *Santissima Trinidad*, the largest battleship in the world.

After exchanging heavy cannonfire with the *Santissima Trinidad*, the *Captain* was nearly wrecked. But Nelson steered his ship to another enemy vessel, the *San Nicholas*. As the ships crashed, Nelson leaped on board with some of his crew. Brandishing swords and pistols, they fought their way on to the quarterdeck and forced the Spanish captain to surrender.

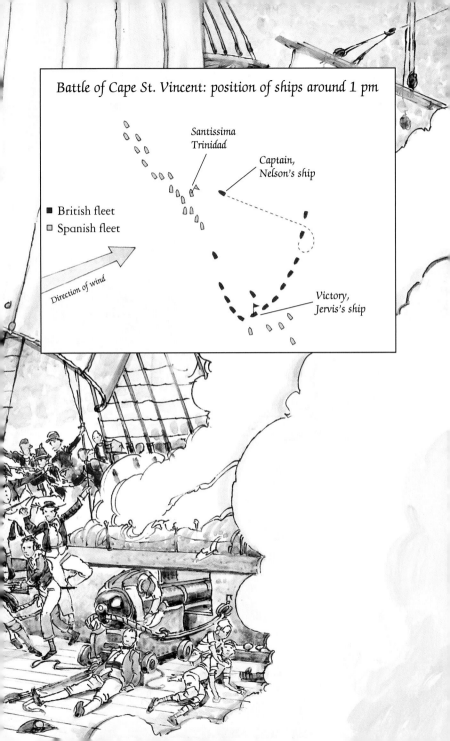

Battle of Cape St. Vincent: position of ships around 1 pm

Santissima
Trinidad

Captain,
Nelson's ship

■ British fleet
□ Spanish fleet

Direction of wind

Victory,
Jervis's ship

Next, Nelson crossed over the *San Nicholas*, climbed aboard the Spanish ship beside it and took control of that ship, too. The British fleet soon began to gain the upper hand. They seized two further Spanish ships and won a magnificent victory for Britain.

When the story of the Battle of Cape St. Vincent reached home, Nelson became a national hero. To board an enemy ship was one thing, but to cross one enemy ship and board a second was a truly extraordinary feat. Nelson was made a Knight and promoted to Rear Admiral.

Chapter 6

Wounded at Tenerife

Nelson was soon back in action against Spain, off the coast of the Spanish island of Tenerife, in the Canary Islands. One evening, he led a raid on the port of Santa Cruz in a flotilla of smaller boats. As Nelson approached, the Spanish opened fire and a musket ball hit his right arm. His stepson, Josiah, was on board and helped to row him to his ship.

"It's no good, my arm's quite useless," Nelson gasped to the ship's surgeon. "You'll have to cut it off."

Surgeons often performed instant amputations in the middle of a battle. It was a quick way to prevent infection spreading to the rest of the body.

The doctor lay Nelson on a table, collected his knives and saws and began. But there was no anesthetic, so Nelson was held down by sailors as the surgeon sawed through his arm.

Despite his pain, Nelson was back at work that same day, discussing plans and dictating letters. The attack on Tenerife had been a failure, and added to this, Nelson now only had one arm. He feared his career was over. But Admiral Jervis, now Earl St. Vincent, wouldn't hear of it.

When Nelson finally arrived back home again in 1797, he received a magnificent welcome for his bravery at Cape St. Vincent. Fanny was delighted to see him, but shocked by how much he had changed. His hair had turned white, his right eye was almost blind and several of his teeth were missing.

He was also in constant pain from his arm, which wasn't healing properly. Fanny immediately devoted herself to nursing him back to health.

Meanwhile, Napoleon had taken control of the Mediterranean and Britain was on constant alert against an invasion from France. It wasn't long before Nelson was sent to sea again, to keep watch over the French fleet.

Off the French port of Toulon, he discovered a fleet of ships preparing to sail with thousands of soldiers on board.

"Napoleon's planning another battle," Nelson told his officers. "We must find out where. Spain, Portugal, Naples... or England?" And he ordered his crew to watch the port, day and night.

Then a terrible storm struck. Vast waves hurtled over the sides of the ship and the wind raged, bringing masts, sails and rigging crashing down.

When at last the sea grew calm, Nelson picked up his telescope to examine the port. What he saw astounded him. The port was empty.

"I don't believe it," Nelson roared. "They've escaped!"

A passing ship reported the French had been sighted sailing east.

"So where are they heading?" Nelson wondered. "I must find out."

Chapter 7

The Battle of the Nile

Nelson felt sure that Napoleon was heading for Egypt, from where the general could sail to the Red Sea and disrupt Britain's trade route to India. So he ordered his loyal captains to set sail for the Egyptian port of Alexandria.

But when the British fleet arrived, there was no sign of any French ship. Nelson grew anxious. Since he'd allowed the French ships to slip away from under his nose, his whole career rested on finding them again. He led his fleet to Greece, but after receiving reports from spies they headed back to Egypt. His captains followed, but many sailors were losing patience.

"How could Nelson allow an entire fleet to escape?" asked one sailor. "If we don't find them, he's done for."

"Maybe he's past it," said his friend.

At last, on August 1 1798, the French warships were sighted, anchored in a heavily defended line in Aboukir Bay, near Alexandria. On Nelson's ship, the *Vanguard*, the band played and sailors danced. Meanwhile, Nelson drew up his plans of attack.

At five o'clock that evening, Nelson signalled to the fleet: "Prepare to attack the enemy."

Nelson had noticed that the French

ships weren't ready to fight on their side facing land. If some of his ships could squeeze behind the French, avoiding the rocks near the shore, they stood a good chance of winning. On every ship, preparations were made for the fight ahead. Decks were cleared and guns heaved into position.

Just before sunset, the captain of the British ship, *Goliath*, steered up to the French fleet and sailed behind them, along the coastline. He was followed by four other British ships. The French, with no guns ready to fire on that side, were powerless to stop them. The rest of the British fleet attacked from the front.

The battle had been raging for two hours, when Nelson – studying a map on the quarterdeck – was hit by cannonfire. He was thrown across the deck, blood pouring from his forehead. As he lay there, badly dazed, sailors rushed to take him to the ship's doctor.

That evening, his head swathed in bandages, Nelson watched as flames engulfed the enemy flagship, the 120-gun *L'Orient*. At ten o'clock there was a deafening explosion as *L'Orient* burst apart, sending timber, sails, fire and smoke shooting into the air.

By dawn, the Battle of the Nile was
over – a great victory for Britain. Out
of thirteen French warships, just two
escaped. Napoleon's army was stranded
in Egypt and the Mediterranean was
under British control.

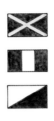

Chapter 8

Lady Emma Hamilton

After the battle, Nelson was in no hurry to return to England. His head throbbed with pain and he found little comfort in Fanny's letters. They were full of domestic worries and complaints about the cold, when instead he longed to hear loving admiration and praise for his wonderful acts of bravery. Besides, the *Vanguard* needed repairing, and the most convenient place to dock was Naples.

The people of Naples, terrified of being invaded by Napoleon, were ecstatic about Nelson's victory over the French. As the *Vanguard* sailed into port, a huge flotilla of boats came to greet her. Crowds cheered while bands played *See the Conquering Hero Comes*. And, as Nelson stepped ashore, hundreds of birds were released from their cages by local fishermen.

The king and queen of Naples came to welcome Nelson, accompanied by Sir William Hamilton. Meanwhile Lady Emma Hamilton excitedly awaited Nelson's arrival at home.

At 33, Emma was a great beauty. She was confident, charming and affectionate, and loved to sing and entertain. In particular, she was known for performing extraordinary statue-like poses for the amusement of her friends.

The second she saw Nelson, Emma was overcome with emotion and collapsed into his arms. Moments later, she and Sir William were insisting that he stay with them. At once, Emma set about organizing a 40th birthday party and victory ball for Nelson at their mansion. In the middle of the party, Emma stood up and sang a song specially written about Nelson, while staring adoringly into his eyes.

As the days went by, Nelson became entranced by Emma and it was clear that the two were falling in love. People began to gossip about them, but Sir William didn't seem to mind. He cared dearly for Nelson and they remained friends.

Meanwhile, as news of Nelson's Nile victory reached Britain, thousands of people flocked into the streets to celebrate. Church bells rang, guns fired salutes, bonfires were lit and songs, dances and plays were written for him. Portraits of Britain's naval hero were snapped up, not to mention countless souvenir mugs and jugs, teapots, fans, coins and even buttons.

Nelson was made a lord, with the title *Baron Nelson of the Nile and Burnham Thorpe*.

Back in Naples, a French army entered the city, helped by local rebels who wanted to overthrow the king.

Nelson helped the petrified King Ferdinand

escape to the island of Sicily. After months of fighting, the French were finally forced to leave and Ferdinand returned. He rewarded Nelson by making him the Duke of Bronte, a town near Mount Etna.

The naval chiefs back at the Admiralty in London weren't so pleased. They wanted Nelson to come home. Not only had he ignored their recent commands, but his relationship with Emma was causing a scandal. Luckily for Nelson, the Hamiltons were also going home, so they returned together. But there was a complication. Emma had a secret. She was pregnant with Nelson's child.

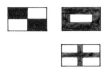

Chapter 9

The Battle of Copenhagen

Lord Nelson arrived at Great Yarmouth in pouring rain, in November 1800, to a welcome from an enormous crowd. Waving from the balcony of an inn, Nelson looked quite a spectacle with medals and stars all over his chest. Emma stood beside him, in a white dress with the words "Nelson" and "Bronte" embroidered on the hem.

By now, Nelson and Fanny had agreed to part. It was clear their marriage was over. Nelson's father was shocked, and so were many people in London society, who refused to see him.

But Nelson had more serious things to worry about. Napoleon – who had recently conquered Austria and made an alliance with Russia – looked more powerful than ever. Worse still, Prussia, Denmark and Sweden were plotting with Russia to stop trading with Britain. This was a disaster. Britain badly needed timber, canvas and iron from these four countries to make battleships. Nelson was made second-in-command of a special fleet under Admiral Sir Hyde Parker and told to prepare for battle against all four countries.

In February 1801, while he was still

anchored off the English coast, Nelson received news that his daughter, Horatia, had been born in secret. Nelson was ecstatic about his new daughter and wrote to Emma two or three times every day.

As the fleet prepared to sail, it was clear Nelson and Admiral Parker did not agree on tactics.

"We must attack the Danes at once and show them what we're made of!" Nelson declared. "The boldest measures are the safest."

"But if they join up with the Swedes, Prussians and Russians, they'll destroy us," Parker replied.

Finally, on April 2 1801, Parker allowed Nelson to lead the attack on the Danish port of Copenhagen, aboard his ship, the *Elephant*.

Nelson steered the fleet into a narrow passage between the Danish line of ships and a large sandbank. It was a daring move, but Nelson was confident of success. He knew that British gun crews were the fastest in the world, capable of firing their cannons once every minute.

There was a thunderous roar from

In the Battle of Copenhagen, the Danish ships were closest to the coast.

the cannons as the ships became locked in battle. In the shallow waters, three British ships ran aground. Parker panicked and signalled Nelson to stop the attack. But Nelson was in no mood for retreat.

"I really cannot see Parker's signals!" he said, holding his telescope up to his blind eye.

Nelson carried on with the attack, demanding the Danes cease fire and eventually a truce was arranged. It was another victory for Britain. The Danish Crown Prince agreed not to attack British ships for fourteen weeks while Nelson sailed north to Russia.

In Russia, the new Tsar agreed to end the trade war with Britain. Nelson's mission had been brilliantly successful and he was made a Viscount. His only thought now was to return to Emma and baby Horatia.

Chapter 10

Victory at Trafalgar

After just two years of peace, Britain and France were at war again. Spies reported that thousands of French soldiers were gathering in the ports of northern France, preparing to invade Britain. It was up to Britain's navy to stop the French fleet from taking control of the Channel.

In May 1803, Vice Admiral Lord Viscount Nelson, commander-in-chief of the Mediterranean fleet, set sail from

Portsmouth on his magnificent 104-gun flagship, the *Victory*.

For the next two years, Nelson's ships guarded the French fleet in the port of Toulon to stop them from leaving. But one night, they escaped. After a long voyage to the Caribbean and back,

H.M.S. Victory, Nelson's flagship
(A flagship carries the commander of the fleet.)

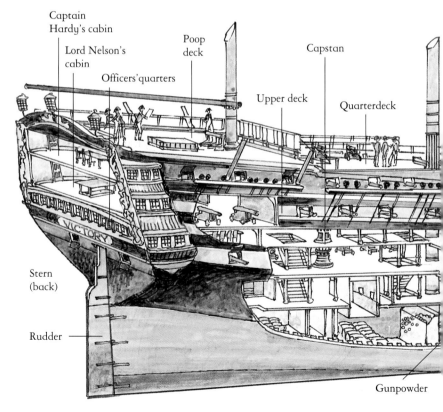

Captain
Hardy's cabin

Lord Nelson's
cabin

Officers' quarters

Poop
deck

Capstan

Upper deck

Quarterdeck

Stern
(back)

Rudder

Gunpowder

chased all the way by Nelson, the French took refuge in the Spanish port of Cadiz, joining up with the Spanish fleet.

It was now September 1805 and Nelson was sure that the combined fleet, under the command of Admiral Villeneuve, was preparing to attack.

Crew at Trafalgar: 821, including 11 officers

Guns carried: 104
Upper deck: 30 guns
Middle deck: 28 guns
Lower deck: 30 guns
Quarterdeck: 12 guns
Forecastle deck: 4 guns

The ship's masts are shown chopped off, but they would actually be taller than the height of the page.

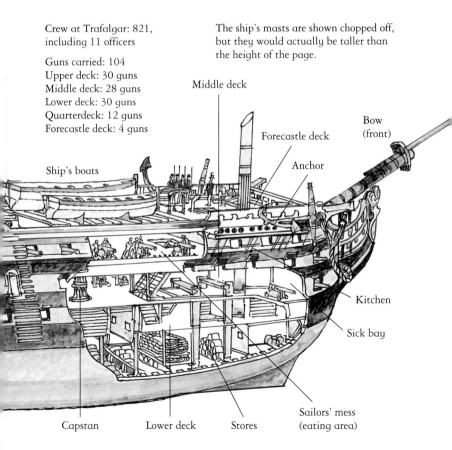

Middle deck

Bow (front)

Forecastle deck

Anchor

Ship's boats

Kitchen

Sick bay

Capstan

Lower deck

Stores

Sailors' mess (eating area)

On his 47th birthday, he summoned 15 captains to dinner on the *Victory*. "The enemy are sure to leave Cadiz at any moment," he declared. "At my signal, we'll attack their middle and rear in two parallel columns. We'll break up their line into small groups and overpower them."

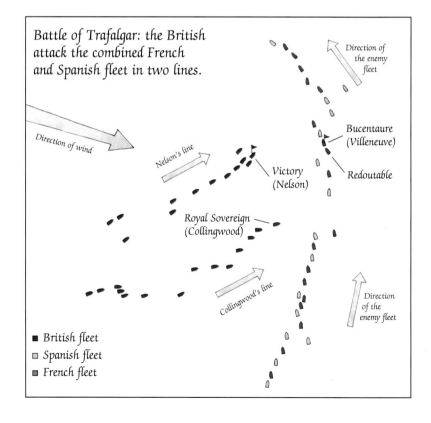

Battle of Trafalgar: the British attack the combined French and Spanish fleet in two lines.

Direction of the enemy fleet

Direction of wind

Nelson's line

Bucentaure (Villeneuve)

Victory (Nelson)

Redoutable

Royal Sovereign (Collingwood)

Collingwood's line

Direction of the enemy fleet

■ British fleet
□ Spanish fleet
▪ French fleet

The captains roared their approval.

On October 19 1805, Villeneuve's fleet set sail for Naples on the orders of Napoleon, now Emperor of France.

"At last! We'll soon have them!" Nelson told his loyal friend Thomas Hardy, captain of the *Victory*.

For two days the British shadowed the enemy fleet. Just before dawn on the third day, Nelson signalled his ships to prepare for a major battle.

Sitting at the small writing table in his cabin, Nelson wrote a will asking his country to provide for Lady Emma and Horatia. Then he composed a prayer in his diary. Shortly before midday, he ordered his crew to signal a message in flags that would inspire the whole fleet: "England expects that every man will do his duty."

At lunchtime on October 21, the British approached the enemy near Cape Trafalgar in south west Spain. Nelson led one line of attack against the middle of the enemy fleet. Admiral Collingwood in the *Royal Sovereign* steered to the back. Then the *Victory* unleashed a devastating blast of cannonfire at Villeneuve's ship, *Bucentaure*.

Redoutable

On the quarterdeck, Nelson and Hardy paced to and fro, watching the action through thick clouds of smoke. With Nelson attacking the middle of the fleet, and Collingwood attacking the rear, the front group of enemy ships were cut off from the action, unable to turn and help their fellow ships. Soon, the British were winning.

Victory

Bucentaure

The *Victory* crashed into the 74-gun French ship, *Redoutable*. The ships were so close that their guns touched and their masts became entangled. High up on the French ship, a sharpshooter identified Nelson's coat, glittering with stars, and took aim. Nelson was shot in the left shoulder and collapsed onto the quarterdeck.

He was carried deep down to the gloom of the sick bay, while up above, Captain Hardy took command.

Later in the afternoon, the rumble of cannons began to peter out and Captain Hardy came to his bedside. "You've won a brilliant victory, my Lord!"

"How many ships have we taken?" Nelson gasped.

"It's too early to tell, but it looks like fourteen," said Hardy.

"I am a dead man, Hardy," Nelson muttered in reply. "It will soon be over."

Silently, Hardy knelt beside him.

"Take care of my dear Lady Hamilton..." Nelson continued in a faint whisper. "Kiss me, Hardy."

Hardy kissed his cheek, his eyes filling with tears.

"Thank God I have done my duty," murmured Nelson as he closed his eyes for the last time.

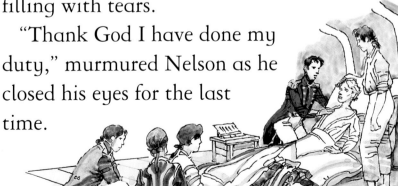

Britain had won an incredible victory. Seventeen enemy ships were captured and one sunk, although only four survived a terrible gale that struck soon after the battle. Napoleon's naval power was destroyed in a single battle and the risk of a French invasion was over. Nelson's body was put in a barrel of brandy to preserve it and taken back to England.

When the news of his death reached Britain, the entire nation mourned the loss of their hero. People wept openly and watched in their thousands as his coffin was carried through the streets of London to a state funeral in St. Paul's Cathedral.

My life at sea

1758 - I am born at Burnham Thorpe, Norfolk.

1767 - My mother dies.

1771 - I join the Raisonnable and then sail on a merchant ship to the West Indies.

1773 - I join an Arctic expedition.

1775 - I see a glowing orb as I recover from malaria.

1777 - I become a lieutenant, sailing on the Lowestoffe to the West Indies.

1787 - I marry Fanny Nisbet on the island of Nevis.

1788 - I am unemployed in Burnham Thorpe.

1789 - The French Revolution begins.

1793 - I am made captain of the 64-gun Agamemnon and sail for the Mediterranean. I meet Sir William and Lady Emma Hamilton.

1796 - Spain declares war on Britain.

1797 - I help defeat the Spanish at the Battle of Cape St. Vincent and am made a Rear Admiral and Knight of the Bath. I lose my right arm during an attack on Santa Cruz, Tenerife.

1798 - I destroy the French fleet in the Battle of the Nile and become Baron Nelson of the Nile. While in Naples I fall in love with Emma Hamilton and help King Ferdinand flee to Sicily.

1799 - A grateful King Ferdinand makes me Duke of Bronte.

1800 - I return to England with the Hamiltons.

1801 - I am promoted to Vice-Admiral and split from Fanny. My daughter Horatia is born. After defeating the Danes in the Battle of Copenhagen, I become Viscount Nelson of the Nile and Burnham Thorpe. I buy a new home, Merton Place, and enter the House of Lords.

1802 - War between Britain and France is over.

1803 - Sir William Hamilton dies. Britain declares war on France, I become commander-in-chief in the Mediterranean and set sail in the Victory.

1804 - I guard the French Mediterranean ports. Spain declares war on Britain.

1805 - I chase Admiral Villeneuve across the Atlantic and back. I destroy the combined French and Spanish fleets at the Battle of Trafalgar, but am shot during the battle.

Lord Horatio Nelson died aboard the Victory on October 21 1805. His state funeral took place on January 9 1806.

Afterwards

Following Nelson's death, his wife Fanny was given a generous state income. Emma and Horatia had nothing. Emma died, penniless, in France, aged 50. Horatia married an English vicar, had nine children and died at 81.

All over Britain, hundreds of pubs, streets and squares were named after Nelson and numerous memorials were put up. The most famous of all is Nelson's Column in Trafalgar Square, in London, built in 1842. Around the base of the 45m (148ft) high column are bronze panels made from melted-down French cannons. Nelson's ship, the *Victory*, was restored and can be visited in Portsmouth dockyard today. And once a year, on the anniversary of Trafalgar, officers and sailors of the Royal Navy drink a toast to Horatio Nelson.

Internet links

For links to websites with quizzes, activities, pictures and more information about Nelson, go to the Usborne Quicklinks Website at **www.usborne-quicklinks.com** and type the keyword **Nelson**.
Please note that Usborne Publishing cannot be responsible for the content of any website other than its own.

Nelson's message

Finally, did you spot the flags above each chapter heading? They spell out Nelson's famous command:

England   expects   that   every   man

will   do   his   duty